Greek Mythology

A Guide to Ancient Greece and Greek Mythology including Titans, Hercules, Greek Gods, Zeus, and More!

Table Of Contents

Introduction 1
Chapter 1: Ancient Greece 2
Chapter 2: Introduction to Greek Mythology 9
Chapter 3: The Olympians 11
Chapter 4: The Titans 16
Chapter 5: Heroes, Heroines, and Other Creatures 21
Chapter 6: Popular Stories 24
Conclusion 26

Introduction

I want to thank you and congratulate you for downloading the book, "Greek Mythology".

This book contains helpful information about Greek mythology, and all of the greatest Ancient Greek tales and beliefs!

You will learn about the different Gods and Goddesses, and what each of them was famous for. You will also discover the different bloodlines, and who fathered who.

This book will explain to you the key facets of Greek mythology, and will take you through some of the best Ancient Greek stories!

You will learn stories of the most famous Gods, monsters, heroes, and Demi-Gods throughout Greek mythology!

Many of today's movies and books have been inspired and impacted by Greek mythology. These stories have been famous for thousands and thousands of years, and for good reason!

Thanks again for downloading this book, I hope you enjoy it!

Chapter 1:
Ancient Greece

An Introduction to Ancient Greece

Ancient Greece is referred to as the *"Cradle of Western Civilization"*. A mountainous peninsula, this is where democracy was first created. It is also the source of many great stories and advancements in philosophy, science, math, and medicine.

The ancient eras, Classical and Hellenistic are considered to be the most splendid of all. These two eras have given the world wonderful concepts, ideas, and art that became the very foundation of western civilization.

The history of ancient Greece is divided into six major eras: Stone Age, Bronze Age, Dark Ages, Archaic, Classical, and Hellenistic.

The Stone Age

A skull found in the Petralona Cave in Halikidiki is the earliest evidence of life. While historians have found it hard to give the exact date of its existence, their estimate is that the cranium is probably 300,000 to 400,000 years old. The skull is classified as a hybrid of the *Homo erectus*, the first hominid to migrate to Africa, and the *Homo neanderthalensis*, the early human inhabitants of Europe and the North East before the *Homo sapiens,* our own species, came into existence.

The earliest evidence of commerce and burials in Aegean has been discovered in the Franchthi cave in the Argolid that date back to 7250 BCE. Stone tools were unearthed in various locations in Macedonia, Peloponnese, Thessaly, and Epirus.

These stone tools prove the existence of Mesolithic and Paleolithic communities in the mainland.

There were Paleolithic open sites discovered in Macedonia, Epirus, and Peloponnese. However, there have also been Neolithic and Mesolithic evidence found.

The unearthing of the settlements of Sesklo and Dimini prove that the Stone Age inhabitants of Greece were able to reach a high level of development during 3000 BCE with complex structures and advanced economies.

The Bronze Age

This period lasted for about 300,000 years. During those years, major economic, social, and technological developments made Greece the center of activities in the Mediterranean. There are three civilizations that historians use to identify the people of the Bronze Age.

The Cycladic civilization inhabited and developed the islands of the Aegean. These people were referred to as the Cyclades. The Minoans inhabited the island of Crete. The civilization that stayed in the mainland is called the Helladic civilization. The Helladic civilization existed towards the end of the 11th c. BCE, also known as the *Age of Heroes* because this is where Greek mythology heroes and epics, including *Hercules,* the *Iliad and the Odyssey* came from.

All these three civilizations had similar characteristics, in addition to having distinct dispositions and culture. For instance, the Minoans are said to be the first advanced civilization in the whole of Europe, while the Mycenaean culture influenced the language and was later referred to as the great splendor of Classical Greece.

The Mycenaeans, using either force or fortune, were able to outlast both the Cyclades and Minoans. By the end of the 10th c. BCE, the Mycenaenas had extended their influence over the mainland, the large island of Crete, and the islands of Aegean, the Ionian seas, and the coast of Asia Minor. It was only after the 1100 BCE that the Mycenaean civilization ceased to exist, either as a result of foreign invasions or internal struggles, or both. It was never clear what caused the downfall. What historians do know is that the extensive damage that had befallen the Mycenaean civilization took almost 300,000 years to repair. This is referred to as the Dark Ages of Ancient Greece.

The Dark Ages

The Dark Ages saw old major settlements being abandoned, except Athens, and the population dwindling in numbers. During these 300,000 years, the Greeks lived in smaller groups that were constantly moving, in accordance with the pastoral lifestyle and livestock needs. There were no written record left to document these years and historians are made to believe that the inhabitants during those years were illiterate.

During the later years, probably between 950 and 750 BCE, the people were able to learn how to write again, only this time, using the Linear B script that was introduced by the Mycenaeans. It was also during this time that the alphabet was first used by the Phoenicians, making changes in the fundamental way of writing by adding vowels to the alphabet. The Greek alphabet is actually the base from which the English alphabet that we know today was formed.

Life for the Greeks was difficult during the Dark Ages, yet historians cite one major benefit of that dark period: the cessation of the old Mycenaean economic and social structures that strictly classified the inhabitants according to hierarchy and heredity, and instead, was replaced with new socio-political institutions that paved the way for the rise of democracy during the 5th c. BCE Athens.

The most significant events that happened during this period were the launch of the Olympics in 776, and the introduction of epics like the *Iliad* and the *Odyssey* by Homer.

The Archaic Era

The Archaic era lasted for about 200 years, 700 to 480 BCE. It was during this time that the epoch population of Greece recovered and became politically organized. The city states, Polis, consisted of a combination of the local, foreigners, and slave inhabitants. This kind of social organization needed developments in the advanced legal structure that would ensure the smooth coexistence of the different classes and equality among the economic status levels. This was the precursor for democracy which came to be 200 years after in Athens.

Having dominated trade and commerce in the Mediterranean, and extensive expansion of businesses overseas, several cities emerged as cultural centers, like Athens, Corinth, Sparta, Syracuse, Thebes, Halicarnassus, and Miletus, among others.

Classical Greece

Classical Greece is considered the period of maturity followed the Archaic Era. During the period of 480 to 323 BCE, Sparta and Athens dominated the Hellenic world with achievements in the military and their culture. Both cities rose to power using alliances and reforms, not to mention a series of victories against the Persian armies.

The long war ended when Athens and Sparta ceased to exist and a new dominant power in Macedonia began to rise. City-states Thebes, Syracuse, Corinth, and Miletus all played major roles in giving Classical Greece a lot of cultural achievements.

Athens introduced to the world the principles of democracy. Classical Greek thinkers dominated for thousands of years. In fact, their principles are still relevant up to this day. The teachings of Aristotle, Plato, and Socrates became the reference points for countless thinkers of the modern world.

Hippocrates became known as the *Father of Modern Medicine*. His Hippocratic Oath is still in existence today. The comedies of Aristophanes and the dramas of Euripides, Aeschylus, and Sophocles are considered masterpieces.

Alexander the Great, son of King Philip II fulfilled his father's ambitions of conquering nations beyond the borders of Greece. His numerous victories in the battlefield earned him the name *the Great*. He was not only a great leader but also a charismatic one, and he used these two qualities to triumph over his conquests.

The many conquests of Alexander the Great changed the course of ancient history. The Greek territory expanded to Eastern Mediterranean, to as far as Asia Minor, thus influencing a plethora of cultures that paved the way for the emergence of the Hellenistic culture after his death.

The Hellenistic Era

This age marked the transformation of Greece to an open, cosmopolitan, and exuberant culture from introverted and localized city-states. Their influence transcended to the whole of the eastern Mediterranean area, reaching as far as Southwest Asia.

The Greek language was established and became the official language of the Hellenistic word. Art focused on the *Real* instead of the *Ideal*. Man was depicted in art and literature as exuberant. Themes expanded from the daily life to the emotional world of gods, heroes, and humans.

Since Alexander the Great did not leave any heir, the Hellenistic Period saw the emergence of different rulers and kingdoms, and three major kingdoms were established after his death.

Ptolemy ruled Egypt and some parts of the Middle East, Seleucus became the head of Syria and the remnants of the Persian Empire, and Antigonus with his son, Demetrius, controlled Thrace, Macedonia, and northern Asia Minor. There were smaller kingdoms that existed, like the Attalid kingdom of the Pergamum in eastern Asia Minor, and kingdom Bactria, an independent kingdom established after the Diodotos-led rebellion of the Greeks against Seleucus.

A lot of thinkers and artists emerged during this era, including the Skeptics, the Epicurians, and the Stoics. Public buildings and monuments were constructed.

By the end of the Hellenistic Era, the Romans had become a formidable power. In 200 BCE Rome had occupied Italy, Illyria, and the entire coastal Adriatic Sea. In the 2nd Punic War (218 – 201 BCE), Hannibal of Carthage successfully led the Greeks in fighting the Romans in Italy. With the help of Philip V of Macedon, they were able to take Illyria and eventually took Greece from the Romans.

In the end, however, the Hellenistic kingdoms disappeared as old rulers died and control was given to the Romans.

It was the Battle of Actium that many historians consider as the pivotal moment that signaled the end of Ancient Greece. After that war, the whole of Hellenic world was under Rome. Over the next 200,000 years, Greece was to undergo a series of conquests, but came into its own in the 19th C. CE.

Chapter 2:
Introduction to Greek Mythology

Mythology was a huge part of the culture of Ancient Greece. Greek mythology is a collection of myths and teachings about Greece's rich traditions and spiritual beliefs. Stories about their gods, heroes, and monsters, including the nature of the world and the origins of their own ritual practices are depicted.

Greek mythology is clearly embodied in a collection of narratives and in Greek representation arts, like paintings and sculptures. The stories attempt to explain how the world came to be and how people of the ancient world lived. They aim to show the adventures of the many gods and goddesses, heroes and heroines, and other mythical creatures. The accounts were initially in the form of oral-poetic traditions, until there came written copies that became a part of Greek literature.

You might be familiar with two of the most famous poems from Homer, *Iliad* and *Odyssey*. There is also the story of the Trojan War.

Greek mythology has stories about the adventures of Greek gods like Zeus, the king of all the gods; Hermes, the god of travel, hospitality, and trade; Apollo, the god of poetry, music, knowledge, and prophesy; and Poseidon, the god of the sea. There are also stories about goddess such as Hera, the queen of the gods and goddess of women and marriage; Athena, the goddess of wisdom; Aphrodite, the goddess of love and beauty; and Demeter, the goddess of agriculture.

There are also stories about heroes and titans, like Heracles and Prometheus. Other popular stories are about Midas, the king with the golden touch; Pygmallion, the king who fell in love with a statute; and Arachne, the arrogant weaver who was turned into a spider. Monsters and other creatures are also a constant character in Greek mythology, like Pegasus, the horse that can fly; the Sphinx, half woman, half lion; and the Cyclopes, monsters with only one eye.

These stories and their characters, plus the themes and lessons that everyone can derive from Greek mythology helped shape the Greek arts and literature for thousands of years.

In the succeeding chapters, you will learn more about the gods, goddesses, heroes, monsters, and other creatures.

Chapter 3:
The Olympians

The Greeks had 12 great gods that they worshipped and prayed to. They were known as the Olympians. They governed over all humans on earth. They were Zeus, Hera, Ares, Apollo, Aphrodite, Artemis, Athena, Dionysus, Demeter, Hermes, Hephaestus, and Poseidon.

Zeus – Ruler of Olympian Gods and God of the Sky

Zeus is the counterpart of Jupiter in Roman mythology. He overthrew his father, Cronus, the god of time. He won over his brothers, Hades and Poseidon through drawing of lots to succeed his father as ruler of both heaven and earth. His weapon is a thunderbolt. He married his sister, Hera, the supreme goddess and patron of marriage and childbirth, but he had many affairs.

As presiding deity of the universe, he was regarded by the Greeks as the god of all natural phenomena. By shaking his aegis, storms or intense darkness occurred. Thunder rolls, rains, or lightning flashes come at his command.

He was also the lord of state-life. He was the creator of kingly power. He was known as the upholder of all institutions connected with the state.

Zeus was also recognized as the father of men. He rewarded men who upheld the truth, charity, and uprightness, but punished those who sow cruelty and perjury. He was wise and merciful.

The Greeks believed that his home was at the top of Mount Olympus, located between Thessaly and Macedon. The summit was hidden with thick clouds and mist. This was believed to be a mysterious region that even birds weren't able to reach.

Hera – The Olympian Queen of the Gods

Hera was the wife of Zeus. She was also the goddess of women and marriage and the goddess of the sky and starry heavens. She was the eldest daughter of Cronus and Rhea, so she is also the sister of Zeus.

Ares – God of War

Ares was also known as the god of battle-lust, manly courage, and civil order. He was the son of Zeus and Hera. He had an adulterous affair with Aphrodite, wherein they were trapped in a net set up by her husband, Hephaistos.

He killed his rival for Aphrodite's affection, Adonis, while disguised as a boar.

Poseidon – God of the Sea

Poseidon, brother of Zeus and Hades, was also the protector of all aquatic features. He married Amphitrite, who was one of the granddaughters of the Titan Oceanus. He used to desire his sister, Demeter, the goddess of grain, corn, and harvest.

He had the power to command destructive tempests, hurricanes, and destructive mists. He can both create angry waves and sooth troubled waters. Because of this power, he was often invoked by those who travelled by sea.

His weapon is a trident or fisherman's fork, which he used to create earthquakes, raise up islands from the sea, and create wells to spring forth out of the ground.

His home was at the bottom of the sea, a beautiful place called Aegea in Euboea, but he was also a resident of Mount Olympus. However he only went up to Mount Olympus when his presence was requested at the council of the gods.

Apollo – God of Music

Apollo was the son of Zeus and Leto. He had a twin sister, Artemis. He became the god of music because he was always seen playing with a golden lyre. He was also recognized as the archer and he had a silver bow. He was also the god of healing, the god of light, and god of truth.

One of his tasks was to move the sun across the sky by harnessing his four-horse chariot. He was considered an oracular god since he was the prophetic deity in the Oracle in Delphi. Many people from around the world travelled to find out their future, though Pythia, his priestess.

Apollo was also worshipped as a god in Delos, an island originally dedicated to Artemis. As he was the god of healing and medicine, he could also bring upon plagues and diseases to anyone he shot his arrows to.

Dionysos – God of Wine, Vegetation, Pleasure, and Festivities

Dionysos was the son of Zeus and Semele, daughter of Cadmus from Thebes. He was said to have been born out of Zeus' thigh and was taken care of by Ino, Seilenos, and Nysiades.

Hephaistos – God of Fire

Hephaistos was also known as the god of stonemasonry, metalworking, and the art of sculpture. He was the son of Zeus and Hera. He was the husband of Aphrodite. He was said to have been banished from Olympus at birth by Hera.

He was also known to have crafted the first woman, Pandora, under instructions from Zeus.

Hermes – God of Animal Husbandry

Hermes was the son of Zeus and Maia, the daughter of Atlas. He was also known as the god of travel, roads, trade, heralds, hospitality, thievery, cunning, writing, language, astronomy, astrology, and persuasion.

He was known as the personal herald of Zeus.

Athena – Virgin Goddess of Reason, Intelligent Activity, Arts, and Literature

Athena was the daughter of Zeus. She was said to have sprang from her father's forehead, full grown and clad in armor. There are vague stories that Metis was her mother. It was said that Zeus swallowed Metis out of fear that she would give birth to a son that would become mightier than him.

She was a fierce and brave woman that many associated with war. But she only joined wars to defend her state and home. She was known as the patron of their city, agriculture, and handcraft. She was the one who invented the bridle, which men used to tame horses. She was also identified as the creator of the flute, trumpet, rake, plow, pot, yoke, chariot, and ship.

She was her father's favorite child. She was the only child who was allowed to play with Zeus' weapons, including the thunderbolt.

She was the perfect embodiment of wisdom, reason, and purity. She was often seen with an owl, the bird which became the symbol for wisdom and intelligence.

She was made the patron goddess of Athens upon defeating Poseidon in a contest.

Artemis – Goddess of Chastity, Virginity, the Moon, the Hunt, and Natural Environment

Atermis was the daughter of Zeus with Leto, a Titan goddess. She was the twin sister of Apollo. She helped her mother give birth to her twin brother, thus becoming the protector of labor and childbirth.

She asked Zeus to give her eternal chastity and virginity. She devoted her time to hunting and taking care of nature and rejected marriage and love.

Demeter – Goddess of Grain, Agriculture, and Bread

Demeter was considered to be one of the great goddesses. She was the daughter of Cronus and Rhea, and sister of Zeus. She was the mother Persephone and Dionysus, by Zeus.

Chapter 4:
The Titans

There were 12 important Titan gods: Cronus, Iapetus, Oceanus, Hyperion, Crius, Coeus, Theia, Phoebe, Themis, Rhea, Mnemosyne, and Tethys. There were also four Iapetionides, namely Prometheus, Atlas, Menoetius, and Epimetheus.

Cronus – The Ruling Titan

Cronus rose to power by castrating his father, Uranus. He was married to Rhea. Their children were the first Olympian gods. He swallowed all of his children when they were born for fear of his safety. However, Rhea tricked him into swallowing a rock, pretending it was Zeus. It was Zeus who revolted against his father and the other titans. He banished all of the titans to Tartarus in the underworld.

Iapetus

Iapetus was the son of Uranus and Gaea. He became the father of Prometheus, Atlas, Menoetius, and Epimetheus. His name was said to have come from the Greek word that means to pierce with a spear, hence, he was said to have been the god of craftsmanship. However, there are other sources that identify him as the god of morality.

He was said to be the personification of one of the 4 pillars holding the earth and the sky apart, a role that he later gave to Atlas. He was the pillar of the west. The other three pillars were his brothers, Hyperion, Coeus, and Crius.

Oceanus

Oceanus was the son of Uranus and Gaea. He was married to his sister, Thethys. They had several offspring that were called Oceanids. These were considered to be the lesser gods and goddesses of the sea, springs, and rivers.

Hyperion

Hyperion was the son of Uranus and Gaea. He was the representation of wisdom, light, and watchfulness. He was known as the father of dawn, the sun and the moon. He had three children with his sister, Theia, namely, Helios, the sun; Selene, the moon; and Eos, the dawn. He was the pillar of the east.

Crius

Crius was the son of Uranus and Gaea. He took Eurybia, daughter of Pontus and Gaea. He was the pillar of the south.

Coeus

Coeus was the pillar of the north. The meaning of his name is *questioning*. From his name, he may have also been the Titan of intellect and inquisitive minds.

Thea

Thea was one of the daughters of Uranus and Gaea. Her name is also spelled as Theia, meaning divine. She is also known as Euryphaessa. She is recognized as the goddess of light. She was also known as the deity that gave gold, silver, and other important gems their radiance.

Phoebe

Phoebe, another daughter of Uranus and Gaea, was married to Coeus, her brother. They had two children, Asteria or the starry one and Leto, who was the mother of Apollo and Artemis.

She was often associated with the Oracle of Delphi and the moon. She was also known as the goddess of prophecy.

Themis

The Titan Themis' parents are also Uranus and Gaea. Her name was derived from the Greek word that means *current* and *contemporary*. Stories from Hesiod say that Themis was Zeus' second wife.

She represented law and order. She was the one who formulated the divine laws that govern, not just humankind but also the gods.

She was known for three things: she was the goddess of natural order manifested through the Hours (the Hores, which means the seasonal and never ending rotation of time); the goddess of moral order that is manifested through Eunomia or fair order and through Moires, a representation of humankind's destiny; and the third one, the goddess of prophecy, manifested through the Nymphs and Astrea.

Rhea

Rhea, another daughter of Uranus and Gaea, became the wife of her brother, Cronus. Her name means *that which flows*. She was the one who maintained orderliness in the Kingdom.

She had six children by Cronus: Zeus, Hera, Poseidon, Hestia, Demeter, and Hades. She was the mother of gods, but didn't have many followers. She hid Zeus from Cronus in her temple in Crete, who tried to swallow him just like all their other children.

Mnemosyne

Mnemosyne was the goddess of memory. She was one of the daughters of Uranus and Gaea. She was also considered as the ocular goddess of the underground oracle of Trophonios in Boeotia.

Sleeping with Zeus for 9 consecutive days resulted in the birth of what was referred to as the 9 Muses.

Tethys

Tethys was also the daughter of Uranus and Gaea. She was married to her brother, Oceanus. She was the mother of river gods and 3,000 water goddesses. She raised Hera as her stepchild during the time of Titanomachy.

Atlas

Atlas' parents were Iapetus and Clynne. During the war of the titans with the Olympian gods, Titanomachy, he and his brother, Menoetius, sided with the titans, while their other two brothers, Prometheus and Epimetheus were with the Olympians. Atlas led the battle but lost. As punishment, Zeus cursed him to eternally hold Uranus (Sky) on his shoulders. He was to stay on the western side of the earth.

Menoetius

Menoetius' name comes from two Ancient Greek words, *menos*, meaning *might*, and *oitos,* meaning *doomed;* so his name means *doomed might*. He was said to have been violent when mad that often resulted in harsh actions.

Prometheus

Prometheus' name was derived from the Greek word that means *forethought*. During the war of the titans with the Olympians, he escaped being punished by Zeus, for helping the victors, the Olympians. Prometheus was known as the protector and benefactor of mankind.

Epimetheus

Epimetheus' name came from the Greek word that means *afterthought*. His name is the exact antonym of his brother Prometheus' name. Epimetheus was said to have been the foolish one, while Prometheus was the smart one.

He received Pandora as gift from the gods. They had a daughter they named, Pyrrhra. Pandora was the recipient of a jar that contained the evils of the world. Out of curiosity, she opened it and released them into the world. She tried to close it but only Hope was what remained inside.

Chapter 5:
Heroes, Heroines, and Other Creatures

Aside from the Titans and the Olympians, Greek mythology also has a lot of heroes, heroines, villains, and other creatures. We have listed some of them here:

Hercules (Heracles)

Hercules is probably one of the most familiar ones. He was known to be the strongest of all mortals, he was even perceived to be stronger than the gods. He was a demigod, having a mortal for a mother and a god, Zeus, as father. While he was strong, he lacked intelligence.

Perseus

Perseus was one of the most popular heroes in Greek mythology. It was said that his mother, Danae was locked by her father, Akrisios, in a bronze chamber for fear for his life. Upon finding out that she was impregnated by Zeus, both he and his mother were placed in a chest and sent out into the sea. They were washed out onto the island of Seriphos.

Perseus was the one who beheaded Medusa, a monster who turned men into stone when they looked into her eyes.

Psyche

Psyche was known as the goddess of the soul. She was the wife of Eros, the god of love. She was a beautiful mortal princess but Aphrodite grew jealous of her immense beauty. Aphrodite forced Eros to make Psyche fall in love with hideous men, but Eros eventually fell for her. He brought her to a secret palace but Eros hid his true identity. He commanded Psyche not to look at his face but she was tricked by her sisters, and was forced to look at him. As a result, Eros abandoned her. She searched for him and in the end the two lovers were reunited and got married.

Cyclopes

The Cyclopes were huge, one-eyed monsters. One of the most famous was Polyphemus, the Cyclops blinded by Odysseus.

These creatures were said to have been the sons of Uranus and Gaea. However, according to Homer, Polyphemus was the son of Poseidon.

Centaur

The centaur was half-human and half-horse. The centaurs have the body of a horse and a torso (including head and arms) of a man. They were said to be the children of Ixion, the king of Lapiths, and Nephele, a cloud in the image of Hera.

One of the most well-known centaurs was Chiron. He was wise, modest, and civilized. He had excellent teaching abilities. He was also known for his medical skills.

Medusa

Medusa was the daughter of Phorkys and Keto. She was said to have had an ugly face with snakes on her head instead of hair. Any person who would look into her eyes instantly turned into stone. She used to be beautiful and had golden hair. But she fell for Poseidon and married him. She was punished for forgetting her vows of celibacy. Athena cursed her beautiful hair to turn into venomous snakes. Her skin turned green and her used to be loving eyes were turned into blood-shot, scary orbs.

Pegasus

Pegasus was the popular flying, white horse. His father was said to be Poseidon and his mother was Gorgon Medusa.

Chimaera

Chimaera was a hybrid monster. His parents were Typhoeus, a fire-breathing dragon said to be the father of all monsters, and Echidna, a half-snake half-woman creature, considered the mother of all monsters. The Chimaera had the body and head of a lion, but it also has a goat's head attached to its back. It also had a tail with the head of a snake.

It was a resident of Lycia in Asia Minor. Legends say that it was killed by Bellerophon, mortal son of Poseidon and titan goddess Eurynome, the wife of Glaucus.

Chapter 6:
Popular Stories

Greek mythology is also rich in stories. This adventures of Perseus is one of the most popular.

The Adventures of Perseus

Perseus was Danae's only son with Zeus. His grandfather, Arcisius, Danae's father, consulted an oracle to ask if he was going to have children. He was shocked to find out that his daughter's future son would be the cause of his death. Arcisius lived in paranoia and kept Danae jailed underground to prevent her from being seen by other men.

However, Zeus, found her and fell in love with her immense beauty. Knowing that she was hidden in a cave, he turned himself into a shower of golden rain so he could go to Danae undetected. She bore him a son, Perseus.

One day, Arcisius walked into the cave to find baby Perseus with his mother. He didn't believe that Zeus was the father of the child. He condemned the nurse of Danae to death, thinking that she helped Danae with the affair. Although he tried to kill his grandson, his guilt wouldn't let him. Instead, he put them into a chest and set them out into the sea.

Mother and son were washed ashore on an island called Seriphos. They were found by Dictes, a fisherman, and he took them into his home. Perseus grew up to be a brave and strong man.

Polydectes, brother of Dictes, king of the island, was smitten with his mother. He tried to protect his mother and never left her side. In order to get him out of his way, Polydectes made a plan and invited his friends to dinner. The king asked each of them if he asked for gifts what they would give him. Perseus was part of the group. When it was his turn to answer, he said that he would kill the monster Medusa and offer him her head. Knowing that this would endanger the life of Perseus, King Polydectes said yes and asked him for Medusa's head or else his mother would become the king's wife.

Our hero began to travel for Medusa's head. Having been favored by the gods, Perseus got some help from Hermes and Athena. Being smart, Perseus tricked the nymphs to giving him winged sandals so he could fly; a bag to put Medusa's head; and a helmet from Hades with the power of invisibility.

He used his winged sandals to fly above Medusa. He only looked at her reflection with the use of the shiny shield from Athena. Using Hades' helmet, Medusa didn't see him, so he was able to cut off her head, bagged it, then headed home.

While he was traveling back, he met Andromeda and they fell for each other. However, Andromeda's uncle desired her for himself and decided to kill Perseus. Carrying Medusa's head, he used it to turn Andromeda's uncle into stone. Arriving home, he also turned Polydectes into stone as well.

Meanwhile, Perseus' grandfather heard about his accomplishments. He fled for fear for his life, but fate had other plans. Arcisius was invited to a ceremonial game in Larissa, organized by King Tentamides. Perseus partook in the said event. When it was his turn, the discus fell from his hand, hitting his grandfather, and instantly killing him. When Perseus found out about his grandfather's death, he buried him with honor.

Conclusion

Thank you again for downloading this book!

I hope this book was able to help you learn more about Ancient Greek mythology!

Finally, if you enjoyed this book, please take the time to share your thoughts and post a review on Amazon. It'd be greatly appreciated!

Thank you and good luck!

www.ingramcontent.com/pod-product-compliance
Lightning Source LLC
LaVergne TN
LVHW021748060526
838200LV00052B/3537